Crazy

Legs

By Tony Nesca

<u>Chapbooks</u>

Stale Anchovy Kisses -

Dead Bats Amidst The Bullshit Laughter And The Lovestricken Cockroaches –

Hollow Man –

La Gioconda -

Charlie -

Mondo Cane -

<u>Novels, Short Stories, Poetry</u>

Dishpig -

About A Girl -

Emma Strunk -

Jukebox Music -

La Gioconda (the novel) -

The Do-Nothing Boys -

Bulletproof Smile -

Vodka Orange Sunday -

Hobo –

Crazy Legs -

Crazy Legs

Tony Nesca

Crazy Legs

Copyright © 2014 Tony Nesca

ISBN: 978-1-7752112-8-0

Printed in The United States of America

Published by:

Screamin' Skull Press

screamingskullpress.net

Tell him I'm too fucking busy-- or vice versa."

— <u>Dorothy Parker</u>

If you do not breathe through writing, if you do not cry out in writing, or sing in writing, then don't write, because our culture has no use for it."

— <u>Anaïs Nin</u>

Those who were seen dancing were
thought to be insane by those who could
not hear the music.

- Nietzsche

This is a work of fiction

TEN THOUSAND DAYS AWAY FROM YOU

I went down to Confusion Corner

saw the hip-hop happy parade,

saw the lowdown distant blues,

saw the mad and beyond scream into the
rain,

saw the punch-drunk crying under the
streetlights,

saw the easy going smiles fade into
yesterday,

felt the long warm kisses recede without
warning,

felt the bang-bang purple sunlight of my
brain,

felt the long and distant Canadian Road
trip

wish me ill luck all the way,

I saw the sad and angry thunder-moan

ten-thousand-days in the desert-song,

I saw all of this,

and I felt it too,

but I didn't see you baby,

I didn't see you

...

THIGH-HIGH LEATHER SCREAMIN' VIOLENT LOVE

Like the soft cool breeze in the Tuscan
glory,

you blew long distance kisses

you cried amidst the telephone fuck-
jobs,

and as the sun died slowly

and the morning-after blew the blues,

you screamed violent love

in the thigh-high

leather rhapsody

...

BUTTERFLY EYES

On Garwood Avenue and Mulvey Street

lies the sweet murmur of your

butterfly eyes

the soft caress of your desperate

love-touch

the sugar-cake moonlight kisses

of your undying happiness

and my fading

erection pointed in all

the wrong places

...

ALMOST HOLY

…we used to hang in the Osborne
Village

at the corner of River and Osborne

me and crazy Kenny,

he talking all sorts of shit and the

LSD just kicking in

and street kids riding their doomed

skateboards and crazy Kenny not crazy

at all,

he got that mind-groove bent on
destruction

he peaceful and vengeful and almost
holy

so the streetlights painting the night
orange,

the Mohawk boys running wild and
glory,

the predators easy-hunting,

the Village freaks hungry for so much
more,

the bums begging for truth,

the Buskers adding up to sweet-fuck-all,

and goddamn the whiskey runneth easy

Kenny looking smooth and hippie-
glorious talking

nothing but wine and veritas,

sweet low-down hustler selling us

latest marijuana high-time shivers

we smoke, we watch, we laugh,

grey-haired young lady blows kisses into
the wind,

tough biker type screams in white/light
pain,

street-painter sells his latest groove and

he looks bright and alone and sad

and the world sings in rhythm…

LAZY AFTERNOON

That moment,

that day high on grass and the

soft thunder in the air,

you smiled eternal rain

you laughed sweet darkness

you arched those hips and

flashed those thighs

and I saw your love baby,

and I saw the rest,

your lips spouting golden orange

my love a slow-easy trickle down

your leg

...

TIGER-RAG

Thought I heard the piano do it right

as the flooded Saskatchewan mind-

desert

melted into late-night beer drawl

and

my easy heart

strung in two

can make you cry -

my casual death-march

can make you sing -

alive all at once

sad and grateful and goddamn mighty

mean

SAVAGE MOON HUNGRY

Let me go home baby,

let me run dizzy and wild,

watch your daddy moving along,

watch him laugh and howl,

listen to his glorious death-song crackle
happily,

listen to his thunder-march crisp and
pure,

let me follow that savage moon baby

up and under and hungry like lightning,

hungry like forgotten eyeshade,

clinging to the shadows a waterfall
delight,

watch your papa slink through the
midnight sewage

and listen to the rock and roll rapture
coming in

thick plumes of blue and pink,

ooooooh yeah,

your lipstick drug-running getting me
oh so down,

your mindful meandering whoo-hoo a
crazy sound,

let me croak with the bullfrogs,

let me murder them bloody,

let me ride the lonesome wind-song,

   let me go baby,

   let me go home

   ...

ALWAYS ALL THE TIME

You gotta come into the night cuz

it's alright, yeah,

it's alright,

hear me girl

don't you go that way,

don't you go too

sing it to me nice and sweet

never to end,

oh yeah,

never to end –

hiding in the sweetness of all that

stay with me man,

make it cool like mid-day siestas

make it all mine and yours,

don't you go that way,

    don't you crawl that way,

    there is a bright shining light

    in our direction,

    never to end,

    on the paperboy in the moonlight

    the mailman in the rain

    the politician on his knees

    the astronaut in the sky

    me and you and these four walls

    never to end,

    no way

        ...

WHAT I NEED

Every day,

I see you smile,

every day

I see you cry,

every day

I watch you breath,

every day

our Saturday night grows

deeper and deeper

and our rock and roll desperation

rings forever true

...

UNDER THE WINNIPEG TREES

Today,

grass so green and red

sky as blue as shit

there's an old lady over there

she's diggin' me,

under the downtown awnings

people scream in whispers

young punk grins like hell

falafel vendor hands out change,

blue-man hollow

he mean and rusty

sun up high and lonely

trees collide and the shade moves in like

hunger

so sick and tired

so lean and blind

invisible to your touch

desire running wild,

wild like honey-scream los angelos

wild like whiskey Napolitano

wild like me and you on wine and rum,

wicked peasant girl wishing for more

grandma moses smiling murder

she's diggin' me,

summer park on the corner young

people laughing sunshine

cuz ain't nothing sacred

oh yeah baby bye-bye-love,

old lady smiles again making sure the
world

falls with her,

wish I was there,

wish I was forever happy in

the killing fields of my neighbourhood

where beer bottles roll down the street

and the congo-rage runs wild,

yeah, she's diggin' me,

and through the bedroom window

you purred and howled victory

wednesday morning beer draft

easy happiness

fifty cents a day

    at dim-light bookstore young broad

giving toothless grin

    in

    the moon-light

    she sings Barbarella under the

    Winnipeg trees,

yeah,

under the Winnipeg trees -

today,

grass so green and red

sky as blue as rain

old lady over there smiling pure
evil beauty,

diggin' me no longer

...

JUKEBOX SINGIN' HIP-HOP ANGER

Deep blue jeans and superhero boots

she works uptown-hustle

the stars hang in the air dead and tired

the moon looks like last-drink-harry

she empty-head happy

heart full and distant

blonde hair curls around the room

Beelzebub late for happy-hour

stranglehold got ya singin' baby

and the sun just sits there doing nothing

and the gloom hangs in the air then falls

like easy

moonshine,

she not-knowing and knowing full-well

baby

got spoonful of fun

got easy laughter teardrops,

deep blue jeans and superhero boots

jukebox singing hip-hop anger,

"hey man" she says, "why don't you

come over here

for a minute"

    "on no baby" I say, "oh no, ain't got

noooooooooooo time for trouble"

    "uh-huh" she says,

    laugh like anaconda in your bed

    like the sky smiles no more

    like the piano screams in agony

    like love is all around

    but too far away for you...

WHEN THE RAIN IS HEAVY AND WILD

When the rain is heavy and wild

you walk the streets shining and grey

the music soaked through gleams deadly

moments torn from your sunshine-
memory

and the sweetest smile -

you think heavy glory under the brick-
house awnings

water pelting away up-top,

that high saxophone hangs in the air

then the piano eases its way in,

and the barroom tremors cling like
shadows

their gloom making it just right -

another one for me, jack, you

say in the wild of the moment

another sing-a-long beat happy rumble,

crazy young girl in the deep blues of
your night

she's doing it on the bathroom floor
baby

blissful and tragic and forever laughing
—

the unreal happiness sets in with long
easy bursts

you crouch low brain washed down in
sombre yellow

teeth bashing an uneasy truce

and what a sad-beautiful sound it all

makes

don't it?

when the rain is heavy and wild

you walk the ragged streets

soaked all the way through with that

forlorn music

torn from your best sunshine-memory…

EVERY FRIDAY NIGHT AT THE WINDSOR HOTEL

The blues band kicked in at

10 o'clock,

lights went down

cigarette smoke thick in the air

she hit the dance floor

those hips moving just right

those legs kicking high

that grin from the dark side

crowd howling cuz problems gone

just for the night

gone and lost in the smell of beer and

laughter

and bad-money hook-ups

then came her partner

big man, big gut, strong proud and
beautiful

cartwheels into the fray

moves like grease-lighting

faces those crazy hips and shakes -

he moves large frame with cat-drunk
grace,

swings her up, down and around

then another cartwheel,

crowd explodes,

band cranks it out loud and dangerous,

guitar sings a nasty song,

saxophone snarls and hits it hard

and she grins and struts across the floor,

ooooooh yeah,

she made it sing like cool-easy-rain,

she made it moan like afternoon-sex in

the   schoolyard,

and the big man right beside her,

big smile, big laughter

graceful-violence

every Friday night,

at the blues bar on the corner,

yeah,

    every Friday night,

    at

    The

    Windsor

    Hotel

    …

MY BIG MAMA

And I swear,

it came like two-train-running,

like early morning eviction notice

like 24-hour love

like midnight summer movies

like me and you crashing

drugs in hand

one life to live,

and living it hard

...

THE GREAT ANTI-PEACE PROTEST

Don't let it come easy,

oh no,

don't let it come gently,

crash and moan and scream blind
misery

hurl chunks at the sun and all the hippie
sweet things,

make it ugly wrong and all-too-
permanent

like when you bopped old man Friday
under the bad moon rising,

like when you sang out of tune ditties 3
fingers in her underwear,

wrap your tongue all the way into
Tuesday and

    don't let it come gently,

    oh no,

    when the hatred finally ends,

    when the anger finally runs out of
gas,

    when you're all dried up between
the legs

    then the great anti-peace protest can
begin –

        even heaven is crazy

           and far out of reach

             …

100 MASTERS AND YOU

Spent the day with Picasso, Matisse,

Van Gogh and you,

felt the tortured happiness and

heard the streaming colors and Van's

heavy brushes making me crazy amidst

the corn rows

and blue-guitar Pablo grinning like

Memphis Slim singin' like Mattise

studying in the

nude then came Jean-Paul Riopelle

me all dizzy daddy,

me sick with love and lust

and your sad-happy smile

keeping time with your footsteps beside

me

always and

forever

as Francis Bacon moved forward and

dug deep into

our minds,

and

Warhol going blonde on blonde,

Rembrandt groovin' with those

gorgeous fat girls of

his,

Monet too much to bear makes

me want to feel,

makes me want to spin,

makes me want to die,

makes me want to sing,

makes me want to scream

all-out peace love and war baby

just you and me

me and you

and

all

the 100 masters

of the world -

and the hell with the masters,

    you and me will do

    just fine...

GOT ME A WOMAN

I got me a woman

other side of town

she got big-legged blues

she got low-lip mustard

she give me all that scaramouche

then she give me some more

well, I reply, I got something

all wrapped up and hungry and

dying just for you,

here's my salvation I say,

here's my body true and blue,

here's what I got when it rains

uh-huh,

when it rains -

this morning ain't got nowhere to go,

this morning got a small killing a-

coming,

this morning I think of you poor old girl

cuz I got me a woman

other side of town

got me a butterball sweet-thing all

juicy and wild,

she got big-legged blues

she give me all that scaramouche

and

ain't got nothing left,

ain't got nowhere to go

ain't got nothing to do

but walk the streets

have a beer or two

go back to my woman

other side of town

...

NERVE JANGLED NEUROSIS

...when the music sounds just right
mean and distant, when the moment
sings loud and upright and blows
straight up your skirt, when something
feels it's easing its way into your nerve-
jangled neurosis you just keep moving
smooth walking down scarred sidewalks
past gloomy brown

early-morning-stories alive with
something crazy in the thin-skinned
queasy funky night

oozing laid back desire hands in pockets
lips whistling that latest tune,

under the shade of the Winnipeg trees

painted houses all red and blue and

green move just slightly sun-beams

whisper

Tuesdays with Nancy Bobbysoxer

afternoon lap

dances neon living rooms shag carpets

broken glass

buried deep, you gotta wonder 'bout

that off-purple

ghost hanging

out in your bedroom just past 2 in the

morning he's

outlived his usefulness cuz he ain't got

shit to say and

really bad hair

let me tell ya,

when you got sweet blue kisses hanging

lowdown dirty

you should be dancing,

and fuck-a-duck if it ain't just so,

if it ain't all living for that one moment

of tenement glory and happy tales under

the tree-lined streets and the multi-

colored houses,

all for one and one for all and the hell

with money-hungry music chewing up

my brain and

spitting it out at you

...

EVERYWHERE ALL THE TIME

I'm just looking for a way around the

noise

keep hearing it bang all day

keep hearing it scream all night

outside my window

down the street

on the corner

at the bus-stop

under the lights

by the river

running at the rail yards

in my neighborhood

at my front door

under my pillow

and all over the world

  here it comes again

  loaded with inane laughter

  teeth clenched in fury

  christ almighty

  jesus marimba!

  ...

  it comes from you

  ...

ONE THOUSAND YEARS AGO

Lush green park by the Assiniboine
river

my footsteps slide down the dirt road

move through the drowned grass

trees go by in puffs of green-smoke-
laughing

and yesterday-sadness,

wonder if you do the same,

wonder if you feel the breeze on your
arms

the sun in flashes on your cheeks

your eyes closed to the moment,

wonder if you feel the smile on my face

and my mind alive and well

one thousand years ago

when we were angry and stupid

and oh so right,

when we were young

deep and wild,

alive in the moment

and dead to everything else

...

FROZEN LOVE

On this day,

on this lousy day wind blowing

through ice and snow and last-day-
decision

through goddamn insecure anger

I'm telling ya,

I still hear something happening,

I still hear a deep low-down smile

and that street-corner murder

and your low-down-legs wrapped tightly

'round my head,

and nobody telling you what to do,

and nobody telling you when to die,

cold early morning meetings,

world frozen and true,

ain't nothing more real than

this lousy day,

wind blowing through ice and snow

and your oh-so-angry-thighs

telling me

    we ain't done

    young fella,

    not by a long shot

      ....

THE NIGHT SHINES IN THAT ORANGE STREETLIGHT GLOW

When you look out windows at night

through smoke-clouds and tired eyes

and the night shines in that orange
streetlight glow

and the rain-soaked skyline's barely
visible in the gloom,

when the distant-lost wander the streets

and hatred abounds and the steam from
your hot drink hangs

in the air,

when you recede in your mind and all
things

fade,

when you reach back to happy times
long-gone,

when the deep dark heart of Saturday
night

cuts a swath through your brain,

when you realize some of the things
people do just ain't right,

and that some of those people are just
like you,

and the soft drone whisper says
something ugly,

and that alone smile forms on your lips
in the quiet

happy-dark,

when the sidewalk drinkers bend their
elbows

in the rain,

when me and you lost forever meet

under the boardwalk,

when happiness sits coldly just around

the corner,

when puff number 23 feels mad and

brilliant and the words come easy,

when the lost and righteous find

something to do and touch themselves in

all the right places,

the moment shines bright,

for us,

for you,

and the long cool night is alive

as you realize

that everything -

everything

tastes better

after midnight

TOO LAZY TO WORK, TOO NERVOUS TO STEAL

Looking for a job just too damn sad

day better spent leaning up against

streetlight

puffing on smoke thinking 'bout

Claudia and her big-legged-blues

and that crazy skirt crazy thighs

watching motorcycle street-kids

doing their thing and trouble hanging

right around my shoulder

cuz

    I goin' home

    Yeah

    I goin' home

To do my baby

Yeah

Goin' home,

gimme back my pride man

ain't looking for no job today,

me diggin' these young bucks

just groovin' and smilin'

me watching my beard grow longer

and my happiness sticking around

my cigarette smoke trailing off

my easy conversation

empty pockets

no money

no worries just for the moment

cuz

   I goin' home,

Yeah

I goin' home

To do my baby

Yeah

Goin' home -

not robbing no corner store today
man
not hurting nobody in the smiling sun
just going to lean up against this here
lamp-post and dig the small-time
trouble
jean shorts looking groovy and mean
red lipstick bright-mind shivers
even the smart-phone idiots glued to
their non-reality looking alright in
the afternoon laziness,

robbing and hustlin' just too damn hard

and too damn wrong,

ain't doing no harm today

cuz it's a beautiful early afternoon beer-
buzz

and the sun feels just right

and her hair smells like good-riddance
break-ups

    and I know trouble is just around
the corner

    but it's alright

    cuz

I'm too lazy to work,

    and

Too nervous to steal…

SOMETHING HAPPENIN' HERE

That's where I took a break

on the midnight shift

maybe 3 or 4 in the morning

right by large windows facing urban

scene

working at museum in downtown area,

working the shit like I was a security

guard

meant for fighting -

every morning they came 3 street-people

hobbling through the grass and cement

empty bottles in their hands

stopping, looking around,

stumbling,

framed by jagged skyline in background

summer sprinklers coming on at
intervals

what kind of sweet life is this

I say?

they would slit your throat if they

needed,

they would laugh with you if they

needed,

they would destroy the world in one fell

swoop

if they needed,

just like you ain't it true?

    but at 3 in the morning

    in the middle of all that action
strasse,

    it feels like something big

    is happening,

    something outside of reach

    something sweet and violent and

mean -

    and right by these

    large windows moon up high

    I watch the 3 fuckers fill their

bottles

    and slowly, very slowly

    move on down the road…

RIBS AND BALLS

I got this thing inside that

tells me to just keep

moving,

to keep doing and singing

and killing all things typical,

this thing that smiles gigantic

and cries wild strawberry beer,

this thing that wonders where the

hell is my brain and

what happened to Bixby?

this thing she bright and luvly

and she ugly and angry too,

screamin' and wagging her finger

at that goddamn painted lady

on Sargent and Maryland Street,

and the working class ignorance

rearing its fucking head one time too

many,

and the college student shouting learned

nothings,

and the video-game enthusiast saying

goodbye in big bright colors,

and the middle-aged lava-workers

saying the same old shit,

    this thing inside telling me new-age

thinking

    ain't never going to happen

    cuz

    new-age ain't ever coming,

    but keep singing

    it says,

keep moving away and apart,

yeah,

we all dig ribs and balls

and

to love all things is fine and dandy

but all things can become a real
drag,

so learn how to hate too

it says,

the sweet fine music works both
ways

   ...

THE DIRTY BOOGIE

I wander around in the dirty boogie

watch all the starving lawyers and

heavy-laden

poets,

hey boys, why so down man, why

so damn angry,

see all the young broads doing their

jig just for you?

see all the hipsters moving their thing

just for you?

give me a sonnet old boy

cuz old friend coming to see me

nice and heavy and oh so sleazy,

barman he singing the sad songs

and salesman he missing the brand new

Cadillac,

neighborhood baker he smiling but not

too much,

girl at ice-cream counter she's saying

"balls to you daddy!"

I wander around the dirty boogie

see that upside-down crucifix in the attic

and Mrs. Nelson counting sheep,

can you hear the angry voices,

can you hear the grieving money-count

going straight down the drain?

hold on says bus driver

just trying to catch today's news,

street corner dealer he flipping all

the coins,

housewife addict she cooking flapjacks

cigarette in clenched teeth,

taxi driver playing guitar in

slow-mo-alley he never on time,

can you see the swing music in large
bright colors,

can you see gypsey rose crouching oh-so-
low,

her legs spread far and wide

and singin' the blues just for you...

FOR BUK

Turned 49 years old other day

still writing and putting out

books that no one gives a shit about

and writing songs no one listens to –

at this age Charles Bukowski was

already poor and famous and waging

all-out attack on the written word –

I'm just poor –

and this poem is written in your style,
fucker

cuz I got something to say to you:

well done, old boy,

well done…

END OF THE NIGHT

With the blade dug deep into his guts

spilling out all over the floor

he looked out the window

and saw the ever-lasting beauty

shoot across

the crimson-colored

sky

 ...

FOR MR. MILLER

Will never forget discovering Tropic

will never forget my mind reeling from

blow after blow of subversive genius

and street-corner attack on art,

YES, I shouted,

YES, I spat,

this is it,

this is the moment you've been waiting

for,

this is the moment everything changes,

this moment all the children go insane,

all the working-men starve in the

summer rain,

all the money-hungry fools die with their

boots on,

all the mothers of the world relive their

self-inflicted horrors,

my mind took a turn to the left on that

day

reading Tropic of Cancer

in ghetto park discarded

syringe just a footstep away -

no more singing in the rain

no more academia-drivel screwing up

my mind,

it was time to laugh,

laugh loud,

mad

distant

and forever insane –

and forever in debt

to ya, henry

you weren't fooling, baby,

and neither am

I

 …

ELECTRONIC NIGHTMARE

Are we tired yet?

are the billion dollar movies done,

are the vacant-eyed celebrities finally
dead,

have the video games stopped spawning,

have the 90 thousand dollar cars run out
of poison,

are the no-talent pop-stars ready for
their golden wheelchairs,

do we need another slightly better cell
phone,

do we need to be plugged in all the time,

do we need to be continually preyed on

by marketing as soulless as satan while

drunk,

    you there!

    yeah you,

    with that ridiculous machine glued

    to your hands ghostly blue light

shining

    on your insipid mug,

take a look at that grey sky

and that car exhaust and that poor

fucker standing in the rain -

with heads down into their

portable nightmares

and mind forever shut,

the human race moves forwards

and backwards stuck in their electronic
nightmare

    and no-solution technology,

    and I wonder out loud -

    are we tired yet?

DONE WE WRONG

Three-legged dog runs across the street
–

Bullet cuts through plate glass –

Car exhaust black and greasy –

Bird falls from the sky -

Young woman smiles –

Working man orders another beer –

Fire spreads through the grasslands –

Musician tunes his guitar –

Newborn screams in the West End –

Kid drowns in Lake Winnipeg –

Rocket shoots for the moon –

Old man mourns –

Guy and girl fucking in dark room –

Homosexual happy in love –

Bombs drop on Crimea –

Hot apple pie sits on windowsill –

200 girls cry in Nigeria –

Living inside me smoking in the fields -

WE IS GRINNIN'

Sleep all day cuz

the night shift don't come easy

then slip away for a moment

crash and hide with me

your skin and your hair

and the deep dark sky,

give me some thigh and make it work,

give me your tongue and your diamond

eyes,

I say

you shiver and moan in the headlights

and the working class rattle and tear,

you're too wasted for the straight world

too damn smart for everyone else,

no,

it don't come easy baby,

sleep deep into the day

let the sun go by

touch me in that right place

cuz this ain't no holy-day baby,

bus stops right out your window,

school-kid runs by laughing,

dog barks its idiot head off,

mother of three gone straight-up-crazy

blood right up to her ankles,

don't pay no-nothing to all that,

cuz it don't come easy

oh-no

but

skin to skin,

mouth to mouth,

you and I,

at least for the moment,

we is grinnin'

   ...

ONE NIGHT IN MY LIFE

Got a poem just for you

I say,

used to get drunk 4 or 5 times a week

back in the day

now I got it down to once,

or twice

if the moon shines just right

and that is cool and easy

and that is good

and that is all the compromise the gods

are getting from my sorry ass,

but my wife Izzy sits beside me and

fills the glass

and the ice rattles

and the 7-up fizzes

and I smell the rye, I taste it,

and that too is right

and that too means something

cuz I save it for Friday night

and a date with my Izzy and my

keyboard

and all that rock and roll music,

she smiles wicked and lean,

she drinks her whiskey happy and

mean,

Django Reinhardt in the background,

pot smoke in the air,

" I think Peter Criss is one of the best

rock drummers ever!"

"C'mon, man……" She says

"I don't give a shit if he played with that

pansy band and painted his face…."

"…shhhhh, Django is playing…."

Got our music on random playing

through

one of those digital machines,

whatever the fuck,

tune switches to Louis Armstrong and

that trumpet really does it for me,

and that moon outside looks just right,

and that stain on the carpet makes me
smile,

I lament out loud the passing of records,

the scratching needle, the artwork, the
thick warm sound,

"You say, as we listen to our 7000 song
digital music collection.." Says Izzy,
smiling mischief

"You see…the thing with Criss is that he
faded fast, his prime was shorter than
most, and people only remember what
he became, not what he was…"

"Why is that?"

"Cuz people are stupid…they only
remember the last thing about
something, the closest to

RIGHT NOW, know what I mean?"

"I meant, why was his prime so short?"

"Forget it…any hash left?"

In silence for a while,

in tune with the night,
in tune with the last record store
standing,
in groove with us and nothing else,
we smoke hash
the damn thing hard and heavy
coughing my guts out then laughing
in desperation and that too is right and
easy and my mind feeling like cross-
town traffic and punk-rock violence and
hippie-smiles and black water blues,
"Listen" she says "Want to go
somewhere?"
"Fuck that…"
"Me neither…people aren't bad, they're
not all bad, you know?"
"Yeah, I know…I like people"
Billie Holiday starts singing "in my
solitude"
and we stay quiet again
cuz when Billie sings

the world stops –

Do ya know those moments,
those moments when there's
good music on,
when you're with someone you dig,
when you're pleasently high and
smiling,
then that sad feeling slips in,
and it ain't depression coming,
it ain't even a bad thing,
but you feel the sadness slowly making
its way
upon you,
it's not something specific,
it's not anything wrong with your life,
it's just the knowledge that smart people
have
that no matter how happy,
no matter how good,
no matter how beautiful your wife is,

everything, from the furthest distant
corner of the universe to her drinking
glass on the kitchen counter,
will one day be gone –

I put my arms around her
and kiss her with everything I
got cuz she's my everything,
my early morning cannonball,
my after-sex love-smile,
and then that other feeling comes,
do you ever get it?
that feeling that nothing ever ends,
nothing,
that time is an illusion,
a limitation of our minds,
that this very moment is forever,
that me and Izzy will always sing
and laugh and fight,

and I say it aloud to the gods and to the
scientists and to the philosophers and to
the writers,
you ain't fooling me, assholes
got my own sing-a-long-blues,
and I pick-up my guitar
(got a black Les Paul we call Leilani)
start playing a rock and roll riff,
Izzy smiles putting words together like
machine-gun fire sucking on cigarettes
filling the room with smoke
whoooooooooooooo,
we go on and on,
smile,
frown,
get tired cuz my arms hurt and I'm out
of practice,
then Jerry Lee Lewis blasts into the
room,
it's alright, let me tell ya,
it's alright,

"You'd better put Leilani down, she's
going to start bitchin' any moment now
—"

"Crazy bitch, that Leilani…"
"Is that someone knocking?"
"Might be the cops, holy shit, baby!"
She runs and gets the door,
old friend Barney comes in,
Canadian Native, long hair now gone
gray
in a ponytail running down his back
pushing 50 like me,
pushing joy and bitterness and peaceful
violence all together now
he already drunk and happy though
world has laid it's shit on him,
more rye and 7 and the ice cubes make
that noise,
and we laugh hard and ready,
and we sing like we're crazy,
and we've been best friends since we

were seven years old and trudging

through the love and hate

all this time,

"I think Mick Fleetwood is better than

Criss.." He laughs,

"Why you little…" I say,

Izzy digs him and he digs her and she's

running with the hounds this night

they both singing

smoking

drinking

got Leilani out again we're going

deep tonight,

3 AM Izzy bows out goes to crash

as me and Barney continue,

and the sun comes up,

and we are two soldiers left on the

battlefield,

and when the time is ripe we die happy,

and all money-counters can kiss our ass,

6 AM comes around and Izzy

is back, rubs sleep from her eyes

and pours a Rye,

music loud,

bullshit even louder,

laughter loudest of all,

this is some amazing love, I say

HE put us here to love one another, says

Izzy,

and to have a fucking hell of a good time

says Barney,

and what about all the sadness, I say

I can hear the jazz and the rock and roll

and the classical Motown melt into

the early morning gloom,

this is some

amazing love

and this is

one night in my life

   ...

JIMMY

Damn, that smile was everything,
he had cerebral palsy
went by name Jimmy
and owned
one of those lottery booths in
an underground mall called
Winnipeg Square and I worked for him
in my early 20's living with mama
as girlfriend of 4 years had just dumped
my ass,
and I didn't really give a shit cuz we had
outgrown each other and the
split was cool
but still,
it was one more thing gone,
one more thing different,
one more thing to say goodbye to,

but back to Jimmy -

62 years old,
wheelchair bound,
only one arm functioning,
speech hard to decipher,
but I learned to understand him
perfectly
and translated to the less patient,
he was good-natured, kind,
strong as hell
grey hair parted on the side,
not even a hint of self-consciousness,
we catered to the suits and ties
in business high-rise up above,
two lines in front of us,
one for Jimmy,
one for me,
heard them complaining all day
long about money,
goddamn

money,

always money

one after the other

one as ugly as the next,

all looking cruel,

ruthless

and absolutely charmless –

not enough money,

too much money,

not the right kind of money,

too many taxes,

wife spends too much,

(laughter – applause – bow your head -)

I'd look over at Jimmy

and think about how he couldn't even

bathe

himself,

couldn't walk,

could barely talk

and he'd handle the line-up with one

arm,

man the cash register,
look back at me,
then came that smile
and then my day was okay,
laughing with Jimmy,
jumping jive with my old friend,
riding the back of his electric wheelchair
all the way down the mall,
jump off at food court
and have a coffee in the square
in downtown Winnipeg,
suits, ties, bums and honky tonk wishing
then back to our post -

I really dug him,
we became friends,
conservative disabled man,
young long-haired rock and roll kid,
would go for drinks on Friday after
work,
drank his gin-tonic right out

of a straw

little guy holding his liquor

like a pro,

"who could tell if I was drunk anyway"

he would laugh,

what a blast man,

what beauty can come your way,

what a friggen' trip it can all be,

work day coming to a close

hangover almost gone

beautiful office girls dancing by

their men not far behind,

and Jimmy with his blue shirt, brown tie

spastic right arm

his tiny groovy body

laughing and shakin'

and his

forever smile,

forever

in

my

mind

...

FAR AWAY IN TIME

I can't hide
what is in my skin –

I can't hide
what is in my bones –

I can't hide
what is in my words –

I can't hide
how much I hate you –

For not understanding
the sweet sadness -

That is my mind –

JUST DREAMIN'

Not now,

not so soon,

not when everything is beautiful

not when everything is right

not when everything feels like rain

like cloudy seas of green

like pool hall memories cheap draft

galore

like smoke filled rooms and forever love

not now,

not so goddamn soon,

not when the angels smoke cigarettes

and drink moonshine under bright

kitchen lights,

not when Kafka sits with Hendrix

talking

shit on the corner of Broadway and

Memorial,

I float over a lush forest with the wind at

my back

I can hear the rock and roll in the

distance

an electric guitar rings through the thick

brown/green,

oh no not now I scream

not now

but I'm torn out and away

despite my pleas

and I open my eyes

see my lousy apartment and discarded

cigarette packs,

welcome to the world, they're saying,

welcome back, motherfucker

   .....

FEW TEENS WALKED BY ME TODAY AT A BUS-STOP

Few teens walked by me today at

a bus-stop

one of them saying,

" I hate losers with long hair"

not looking at me,

but directing it at me

cuz I was the only fucker with long hair

in the vicinity,

their ridiculous voices and

ridiculous smartphones

and their empty heads

and god-awful, degrading, self-entitled

laughter

made me snap and I told them,

loudly

angrily

with extreme prejudice

to go fuck themselves –

afraid,
they backed off and bolted
and I immediately felt good,
then bad,
then good again –

still wishing I could have kept quiet,
still wishing I had the class
to say nothing,
still wishing I had the peace and love
inside and was capable of
forgiving and forgetting,
I smiled and wished those young dudes
nothing but shitty
luck all the way
down the line

   ...

CUZ I CAN'T GET ENOUGH

Wish I could play guitar like Jessie
Cook
but here I am banging away
in the dark
and the leads are shooting out
of the end of Leilani like bullets
from a machine-gun,
I'm dressed in blue, red-eyed,
under the influence
and no, I ain't no Mood Indigo, baby,
ain't no Petit Fleur
but I'm swinging with the best of them
tonight
all alone in this dark place
my Leilani purring low and shouting out
loud,
she easy movin' moonlight,
she backyard summer-time drinking,

the empty room full of nothing but us,

the empty room precious and right,

snow coming down outside my window

ice forming around the edges,

I play an E chord,

Leilani responds with a snarl

and I realize,

I can't have enough,

will never let it go,

not age nor time nor

easy livin' hot child in the city

can take it away cuz can't afford to

grow up,

mama oh no, there be golden lights

everywhere,

oh no baby, the streets are made of fire

and

Leilani feels too damn good tonight

alone in this room

these four walls looking just right,

and I wish I could play like Jesse Cook,

but not really,

cuz I dig what I'm doing,

and

can never have enough

not enough

never enough,

can't do it,

no no no ….

GOD, LEROY AND LULU

He buys whiskey and sells it
sees how long it can go and
how long he can bring it,
she's better than that
but not by much
drinks coffee late-night thinkin'
late-night runnin' squeezing, licking,
oozing pain and pleasure a
copy of Brave New World on
the table -

saturday night neon happy
he buys whiskey and there it sits
and there it goes with a girl
named Lulu shaking for her life
big bad boy named Leroy
he pointin' and cursing

hey mister, he says, don't even know her

-

she grins not knowing why
coffee cold she's staring down
a barrel of too-much-love
tongue darting in and out lips
pursed and ready and damn they
cool and mean –

he praying cuz Leroy three steps behind
and he meaning plenty harm
lord oh lord he says
just gimme one more day
just gimme one more love
one more taste
one more life
uh-huh says Leroy
jukebox music swingin' some
Texas Flood and I ain't
got nothing for you son -

she slams her legs shut!
hard and easy ain't doing this no
more she says coffee shop
greasy love and lost memory
bleached and ugly and my
sweet-forever always here
drop of sweat like glistening pearl
curls down her leg
no she says don't got no gun –

and into the breezy lights
they run into each other
rain hanging in the sky
music sweet and distant
Brave New World in her pocket
whiskey shot in his
as coffee-shop fades in the dusk
and Leroy hits the gutter
face cut up like a jig-saw puzzle
and god high up in the

sky

grinnin'

his holy ass off

...

FIORENZA

In Italy 14 years old
just coming out of one
growing-up phase and entering
the next lived in villa
in small town called Gassino
outskirts of Turin
big city lights (born there
in the hot bright sun),
villa was in foothills of Italian alps
mountains just out of reach
rising up all around green trees
as far as eyes can see
and there was Fiorenza
neighbor my age sun-bathing in
red bikini all summer long
houses separated
by link wire fence
me playing soccer in backyard

eyes running all over her

body

and there ain't no Tennessee swing here

or Canadian rock-candy,

she was all Mediterranean greasy and

luvly olive skin making me feel helpless

and wanting,

we hurled insults across the fence

at each other playfully

PUTTANA! BASTARDO!

DISGRAZIATO!

her brown/green eyes smiling at the

edges

her golden thighs full and meaty

her arms long and lean

her voice soft and beautiful to me

just a kid but already digging the whole

man/woman game to be played out

year after year

throughout our entire life

and more,

and us young virgins not knowing
we were already hitting the sheets
with everything but our bodies,
then my 84 year old grandmother
coming out into the yard "Goddamn
Ziggycello!" (in Sicilian) "What the hell
are you doin'"?
something lippy coming out of my
mouth always runnin'
and Grandma chasing me all over
the yard Fiorenza laughing
"Ziggycello, you devil! Says grandma "I
kill you!"

Later on laying in bed
got my Kiss records on
thinking of Fiorenza bella,
time after time
making me helpless,
time after time
making me dizzy,

time after time

keeping me warm at night,

I placed my hand in my underwear,

smiled,

then came my grandmother's voice

from downstairs,

"Ziggy, you devil! Where the hell are my

cigarettes!"

and there went one more moment shot

to hell…

MY LOVE STORY

You couldn't know

how much the sky shines

through you

and your smile makes me quiver

all screwed-up and dizzy,

and maybe I'll tease myself tonight

just

thinking

of

you,

and maybe I'll grease myself tonight,

while

dancing

with

you,

and maybe you'll come ease with me

tonight,

my

brain

inside

of

you,

and maybe I'll swim through muddy

waters tonight,

dreaming

of

you,

and maybe I'll rock this town,

thinking

of

you,

but one thing's for sure,

ain't no sun rising

ain't no beer-a-pouring

ain't no piano playing

ain't no whiskey-a-go-go

ain't no nothing happening

without

you

LET ME TELL YA WHILE I STILL CAN

On that street corner

sun, rain or death

corner of Hargrave and Cumberland

Street

the mob sits quiet

'till the sun goes down

the drunks sleep easy

'till the moment comes round

and the junkies gather their thoughts

while they still got 'em

...

IS THERE STILL TIME FOR MY GETAWAY

The morning is here

the sun is down low

even the generals are crying

but no one cries like us,

you got sweet-nothing moon-drops

as the sky fills with fire,

you got acid rain over Canada

and that's okay,

you got real-life suffering and what

she feels – she feels,

even the presidents are whispering

as their god-smack continues

with century-old shouting

never to end,

yeah baby,

never to end,

she's got a tongue like sandpaper

and it feels alright,

she's got religious warfare

bungled up in her tights,

and here comes the night

and it's okay,

and here comes the man yeah he's

looking high,

when the bombs keep dropping all over

the place

and dirt hits the sky like a pizza-pie,

the moon clouds over and the

devils get drunk

and the children cry

and we roll over easy,

and the bus-driver shits all over

the wheel

and the fucked-up plumber

grinnin' from ear to ear

and the thug on the corner he don't give

a shit

and the corporate rape hustler running

for the door,

and even the stars in the sky ain't happy

as I ask you,

my everything -

is there

still time

for

my getaway,

and will you

come and stay,

till my rocket

comes around

…

Tony Nesca was born in Torino, Italy in 1965 and moved to Canada at the age of three. He was raised in Winnipeg but relocated back to Italy several times until finally settling in Winnipeg in 1980. He taught himself how to play guitar and formed an original rock band playing the local bars for several years. At the age of twenty-seven he traded his guitar for a Commodore 64 and started writing seriously. He has published six chapbooks of stories and poems (which he used to sell straight out of his knapsack at local dives and bookstores), six novels, four books of poetry and has been an active contributor to the underground lit scene for ten years, being published in innumerable magazines both online and in print. He currently resides in Winnipeg.

Screamin' Skull Press
Cutting Edge
Spontaneous
Street-Writing
Novels, Stories, Poems
Tony Nesca
Nicole I. Nesca